By The Way

For a lot that was almost said...

Sarika Nair

BookLeaf Publishing

India | USA | UK

Made with ❤ on the BookLeaf Publishing Platform
www.bookleafpub.in
www.bookleafpub.com

Dedication

To those implicit thoughts, lingered in quiet corners of my mind, holding between pauses and possibilities. To those emotions which stayed unspoken, yet shaped the depth of my silence. To every fleeting feeling that never found a voice. This is for you, by the way!

Preface

Some thoughts never make it into conversations. By the Way is a collection born from those in-between moments, the unsaid, the almost said, the deeply felt. These poems are fragments of emotions, whispers of thoughts that often linger longer than words. They are not grand declarations, but gentle nudges, the kind you hear in your own heart when the world goes quiet. Over the years, journaling became more than a habit for me, but this book isn't just about me, it's about every reader who has ever paused in the middle of a thought, carried a feeling without words, or found comfort in silence. Each poem stands on its own, yet all are connected by a common thread of all the beautiful messy layers of being human. I hope somewhere in these lines, you find your reflection.

And just maybe, you'll whisper to yourself...
"By the way, I've felt that too."

Acknowledgements

To my life partner & To my children
who are the Joy's of my world, for being the calm in my
chaos and the rhythm in my words,
for adding meaning to every pause and punctuation.
To my parents, from whom born my first poem.
And to all those who passed through the chapters of my
life, thank you for the feeling you left behind.
Each emotion, each memory, became a verse.
By the way, this book is a piece of you, brought to life.

Cover page design courtesy: Ananda Das (anandadas_art)

1. You Know It Better

I chose love, and I knew I would bend.
I smiled through every nod and vow.
I agreed, not out of fear or doubt,
But to keep the harmony flowing out.
Some promises, I knew, would softly fade,
Like colours in time, quietly laid.
Not because I didn't care enough,
But because life isn't built on the tough.
I wore the customs like borrowed lace,
Beautiful, ephemeral, just in place.
And though my heart danced its own free tune,
I held their hopes for a little monsoon.
I chose him, not the terms around,
And in that choice, my peace was found.
So if some vows don't stay for long,
Let love, not rules, keep us strong.

2. The Space Between Words

In the sway of sentences, silence speaks,
Not every pause reflects your retreat.
Sometimes it's where truth and trickery meet.
You held your voice, swallowed it whole,
A storm of words still echoed in your soul.
Louder than thunder, your thoughts did rise,
But what if loudness still missed quiet eyes?
A silence stitched into what went unspoken,
A presence felt in every word broken.
Even unspoken, your voice remains
A whisper etched in conversation's veins.
And if the world still refuses to hear,
Let your heart speak bold, steady, clear.
For the loudest echoes don't always roar
Sometimes, they shake the silence to its core.

3. Where I Still Exist

I may have walked away mid-conversation,
Left a room, a chapter, a destination.
But words unsaid don't fade with time
They echo softly, like an unfinished rhyme.
I left the crowd, the laughter, the noise,
But not the weight behind my voice.
A glance, a silence, a half-meant smile
They linger quietly, mile after mile.
Not in frames or scripted lists,
But in the hush where memory twists.
In the warmth of an old folio,
In hearts that hold both joy and pain.
I may have gone from sight and sound,
Yet in spaces between breaths, I can see myself.
In thoughts unspoken, in moments missed
That's where I still exist.

4. A Familiar Stranger

It came like a breeze without a style,
A quiet thought, too shy to claim.
Not quite a voice, not quite a face
Just a shadow slipping through inner space.
It lingered where no words reside,
Between the lines we often hide.
A flicker from an untold sigh,
A truth wrapped deep in a silent lie.
Was it a memory or a buried ache?
A dream we let the silence take?
Some thoughts don't speak, they softly disguise
They live in pauses, behind our eyes.

5. The Weight of Almost Said

Right there, between the breathe and the blink,
When the pause grew heavy and
my heart leaned forward.
It hovered on the edge of breath, a truth aching to be set
free,
a feeling too full to stay hidden, yet too fragile to be
spoken.
My voice reached for it, but something softer, doubt, fear,
maybe pride, pulled me back.
You looked away, unaware of the storm
I had just swallowed whole. And so I smiled instead,
While a thousand unsaid syllables curled inward,
Settling deep in a place where unfinished sentences live.

6. The Inner Voice of Letting Go

While trying to rewrite what was never meant to last.
you carry thoughts like folded letters never sent,
each word etched with a longing that no longer serves
you.
But not everything needs closure in conversation
some chapters close gently, in the silence of acceptance.
The mind seeks freedom,
but the heart keeps tying knots to memories
that have already drifted too far.
And real peace, only arrives when you stop chasing
echoes
that no longer belong to now.
So breathe, not to hold on, but to release
not every voice within you needs to be heard aloud,
some are meant to be felt, and then set free.
Let it go, not in anger, not in regret, but in grace,
because some strings are too long
and some stories too soft to carry forever.
Let it be.

7. Scars of Unspoken

To the Lies You Learn to Live With;
Some lies aren't born from deceit,
but from love wrapped in silence
truths too sharp to set free,
too cruel to land where they don't belong.
So you carry them, like nails hammered
gently into your own mind,
a quiet torment you've chosen to endure
for the sake of someone else's peace.
It aches, sometimes in whispers, sometimes in storms
but you've seen what truth can do
when it falls into the wrong hands.
And so, you keep it locked, not because you're weak,
but because some truths can burn down everything
you were trying to protect.
you bleed inside, quietly, bravely for the good of others,
and the ruin you chose to prevent.

8. You know it's fleeting

Some moments slide like soft sunlight on tired skin,
unexpected, warm, too perfect to last.
You laugh louder, hold tighter,
as if joy could be preserved by wanting it more.
And in those few golden seconds,
your heart starts weaving forever
out of something barely meant for now.
You know it's fleeting
yet your thoughts dress it in forever,
your smile stretches beyond reason,
as if happiness could be tricked into staying.
Because somewhere deep,
you fear this might be the last time
life feels this kind, this full, this light.
So you dance a little longer,
say a little more and pretend time's not ticking
while quietly wishing this moment forgets to end.

9. What I Heard but Never Held

Sometimes you just know not by what they say,
but in the way glances linger a second too long,
in the hush that follows your passing,
in the laughter that bends around your name.
And yet, you carry a smile as if you never noticed,
as if words don't curve in corners you've already seen.
It's not ignorance, it's grace.
The quiet dignity of letting them believe
you're untouched by their whispers,
while you walk ahead, unmoved, placid
at peace with knowing and choosing not to react.
Because some truths are best met
with a gentle smile and a silence louder than words.

10. Solitude within the Crowd

Amid the thunder of voices and clatter of presence,
I dwell in a hush no one hears.
Their laughter, their noise,
their vibrant chaos all swirl around me,
but never touch the quiet I carry within.
They see me with a smile woven neatly into the rhythm
of the room.
But my mind it drifts through distant alleys of thought,
balancing dreams, decisions, and delicate threads of
purpose all at once.
They believe I belong to this moment,
but I walk parallel a silent observer dressed in stillness,
gathering clarity in the heart of disorder.
It is a secret grace to be present, yet far,
to hold a hundred thoughts in the cradle of calm
while the world thinks you're simply there.
And in that gentle dissonance,
I find my truest peace not in the noise around me,
but in the quiet only I can hear.

11. When We Were Still Us

Inner Voice now...
No hands but ours,
no borrowed might,
we carved our way to light
Weren't we rivers carving stones,
we headed ourselves,
we climbed the hills
So tell me now, what holds us low...

12. The Page Calling

There's a voice inside I cannot hush,
It stirs beneath my every hush.
A restless pulse, a silent cry,
That rises each time thoughts pass by.
Even in the calmest hour,
It blooms a wild, unspoken flower.
A flicker of feeling, a sudden ache,
A memory I never meant to wake.
Not every word is meant to speak,
Some truths are tender, some thoughts too weak.
But still, they push and claw and climb,
Begging to escape in ink, in rhyme, in page
I carry this weight in every breath,
A chaos wrapped in quiet depth.

13. Restless Pen

My journal knows what lips forget,
The storm I've not confessed just yet.
It's not a habit, not a task
It's a need behind the masks I wear.
A longing to bleed in curves and lines,
To give shape to all that hides behind.
So I write Not to be heard, but to be whole,
To empty the clutter, to unclench the soul.
For each word written is one set free
A little more of peace inside of me
is in you my darling coop...

14. Unnamed Tears

The tears come softly, without a reason I can name,
not from pain I remember, not from sorrow I can frame.
They rise from a place I can't quite reach,
where words never breach.
No loud sobs, no breaking voice, just a slow release,
a quiet stream that carries some unseen weight to peace.
I sit still, just letting the ache unravel in a way only I'll
know.
There's a strange comfort in the way they fall,
like my heart is speaking in whispers I can't recall.
And though I don't understand the why or when,
something within me feels whole again.
It's not grief, not sadness, not joy, not pain
just a soul in tranquillity after holding too much strain.
And when it's done, I don't feel empty, I feel light, like
I've quietly returned to me.
This is solitude, not loneliness, not despair
but a sacred space where my soul learns to repair.
And in these silent tears I never planned to shed,
I find the peace that no spoken word ever said.

15. The Room I Never Left

I walked out,
closed the door, turned the key,
smiled at the world like I was free.
But somewhere in me, the walls still stood,
unchanged, untouched, quietly understood.
The curtains still sway with yesterday's air,
memories folded into the corner chair.
The echoes of words I didn't say
still linger in the silence of that day.
I've moved cities, crossed seasons,
chased reasons, found meanings
but some part of me remained behind,
rooted in that room I pretend not to mind.
It wasn't the place it was the version of me,
trapped in thoughts I couldn't set free.

16. Did I Ask ?

The ache, the wait, the unfinished line,
the questions that still feel like mine.
Every now and then, I visit again
not with my feet, but with my mind.
And it surprises me how
familiar it feels,
how heavy, how real.
I've grown, I've healed, I've moved ahead,
but not everything we leave is truly left.
Some thoughts don't need a stop or pause
they live quietly inside us, forever & beyond.

17. Echoes of Stillness

I build a fortress of reflection.
I retreat within, where heartbeat echoes
with unyielding truth.
The world outside may roar,
but here I find a sacred calm.
Tears that never fell in anger now cleanse the soul with
gentle fire.
I learn to cherish unvoiced moments
that restore my spirit.
Each breath is a quiet vow to honor
the strength in stillness.
I hold my scars as symbols of battles silently overcome.
Within the hush of my thoughts,
I reclaim the power of self-love.
No one sees the metamorphosis unfolding in my core.
Every silent minute testifies to an inner resolve reborn.
In this fortress of silence, I discover a voice that speaks
without sound.

18. Subtle Sanctuary

In the private haven of my heart, I create a gentle retreat.
Each quiet moment is a sacred sanctuary of renewal.
The clamor of past connections fades into
soft echoes of memory.
I embrace a solitude that whispers promises of
healing and hope.
There, amid tender reflections, I let the weight of others
fall away.
Unseen by the world, my resolve blossoms
in the hush of isolation.
I trade clamor for calm, finding truth in the quiet spaces.
In this intimate refuge, I learn to value
the art of gentle detachment.
I hold close the wisdom of silence,
a beacon against relentless noise.
The sanctuary I have built is both fierce and tender.
It honors my need for self-care without t
he need for explanation.
Here, I reclaim my power in the soft glow of
unspoken understanding.

19. Within the Quiet

Beneath the surface of everyday interactions
lies a depth uncharted.
The weight of unspoken burdens lifts in the
gentle glow of introspection.
In solitude, I unearth a resilience that thrives on
honest reflection.
I relinquish the need for constant connection
in favor of authentic stillness.
I gather my scattered fragments
and forge them into something whole.
Within this quiet realm,
I celebrate the clarity of my own voice.
I allow the silence to cleanse, to heal,
and to fortify my soul.
Here, in the untouched calm,
I find a sanctuary for my spirit.
And every silent moment becomes
a testament to the beauty of my solitude.

20. Unspoken Redemption

In the depths of silence,
I witness a redemption carved from quiet resolve.
I step back from the noise, embracing a truth known
only to my heart.
The echoes of past hurts dissolve into a well of serene
forgiveness.
In this private space, I reclaim parts of me long
overshadowed.
Within that silence, my spirit gathers unspoken power.
The gentle cadence of my breath rewrites a narrative of
hope.
In the sanctuary of my solitude, I discover the art of self-
redemption.
But in every unuttered moment, I forge a path to
wholeness.
I honor the silence as both a balm and a bold declaration.
In the unspoken, I find a redemption as fierce as it is
gentle.

21. Strength of Solitude

Leaving space for raw and honest reflection, a deliberate act of nurturing my soul.
In this quiet realm, I rebuild the foundations of my self-worth.
I shed the layers of expectation to reveal a spirit unconfined.
The gentle quiet nurtures a resilience that words cannot define.
Within the solitude, I celebrate the art of being entirely present.
I find beauty in the moments that exist solely for me.
In every quiet breath, I reclaim what was always mine.
The strength of solitude is both fierce and tender in its truth.
It is in this space that I learn to stand tall, unburdened by external clamor.
And with each silent moment, I honor the power of my own being.

22. Inner Reverence

*The soft cadence of solitude reveals strengths buried
beneath years of noise.
I craft my sanctuary from whispered memories and
tender reflections.
I let the quiet teach me the value of unspoken truths.
In this space, I honor the power of my own unfiltered
emotions.
Each heartbeat reminds me that inner peace is a fiercely
guarded treasure.
The silence wraps around me like a mantle of unyielding
grace.
My soul whispers its secrets, and I listen with profound
respect.
In every hushed moment, I reclaim a piece of my
untamed power.
And within that reverence, I stand whole,
unapologetically me.*

23. Unspoken Might

I won't let the world see the shadows that pull me down,
for in the quiet recesses of my mind, a fierce light is
found.
Deep inside, where silent thoughts gather like embers in
the night,
each hidden sigh transforms into a spark of inner might.
I tread a path of quiet resilience, each step a secret vow
to rise above the lows that the surface would allow.
Though the weight of despair may press on me unseen,
I nurture a silent rebellion with every thought that
gleams.
I embrace my inner voice, the wellspring of all I crave,
transforming every hidden whisper into the power to be
brave.
Fake it until you make it until the facade fades away,
and the truth of your spirit shines stronger with each
day.

24. By The Way

I didn't announce my leaving
there were no final words, no closing lines.
Just a soft retreat, a slow unravelling of ties
that once held more weight than they should have.
I smiled, replied just enough, kept the rhythm, played it
rough.
But inside, I was walking away not out of anger, not out
of spite,
but in search of something softer than the noise.
It wasn't that they hurt me loud, but the quiet cuts the
little drains
the heavy pauses I couldn't explain, the way my spirit
dimmed every time I stayed.
So I made space not to punish, not to teach, but simply to
breathe in peace I had long forgotten I deserved.
No one noticed. No one asked. Because distance in
silence wears a friendly mask.
By the way, I know what I let go.
I know what I chose. And in that choice, I reclaimed a
part of me I never should've handed away...

25. Why Not A New Dawn

The night may whisper tales of doubt,
But morning sings a different song.
Hope arrives without a shout,
Yet its echoes are steady and strong.
No shadow lasts beyond the sun,
No storm outlives the sky.
Hold on, the light has just begun
Tomorrow's wings were made to fly.
Not all is lost when paths turn steep,
Not all is done when moments weep.
Each dawn arrives with something new,
A chance to start, a different view.

26. Mind Your Steps

One step today, then one more,
Even when the path feels sore.
Every struggle, every fall,
Teaches you to stand up tall.
Not all days will feel so bright,
But darkness bends before the light.
Keep moving, slow or fast
You'll reach the place you're meant to last.
Doubt may whisper, loud and near,
But trust the strength you hold so dear.
What feels too far, what seems unknown,
Is waiting for you to call it home.

27. Out of the Maze

Lost within my tangled mind,
Looking for a sign to find.
Then I paused and took a breath,
Stopped the race, embraced the depth.
The door was never locked at all,
Just fear that made me feel so small.
Sometimes all we really need
Is faith in steps that set us free.
The walls we build, the chains we tie,
Can disappear if we just try.
Not all who wander lose their way,
Some find themselves along the stray.

28. Strength is Grown

Not in ease or perfect days,
But through storms and endless maze.
Strength is found when knees still shake,
Yet hearts decide they will not break.
Each battle fought, each fear defied,
Builds the armor kept inside.
Not born with fire, but made in heat
Inner strength is self-belief.
The weight of trials makes us rise,
Through tear-stained cheeks and weary eyes.
A soul that bends, yet does not fall,
Is proof that strength can conquer all.

29. When Silence Speaks

Not all answers come in words,
Some are whispered, some unheard.
Silence sings where echoes cease,
Offering moments filled with peace.
In the hush of breath and mind,
Clarity is what we find.
Not every thought needs to be said,
Some are best left softly fed.
Silence teaches what words cannot,
A quiet space where thoughts are sought.
So sit, be still, let silence stay,
And watch the noise just fade away.

30. A Guide in the Dark

Not every star is meant to shine,
Some just guide us, dim yet fine.
The path ahead may not seem clear,
But inner whispers calm the fear.
Trust the voice that speaks so low,
It knows the way, it helps you grow.
Not all who stumble lose their grace,
Some find strength in slowing pace.
Darkness may seem vast and wide,
Yet inside, light will be your guide.
A step in faith, a heart held true,
Will lead the way to something new.

31. Unbound

Not all that stays is meant to be,
Some things must drift, some must be free.
Holding tight to what has gone,
Will only keep you stuck too long.
Let go of pain, release the weight,
Not all closures come too late.
Growth begins when hands unfold,
When hearts stop gripping what they hold.
Not all goodbyes are filled with grief,
Some bring a quiet, calm relief.
What was, will always be a part,
But now, there's space for a new start.

32. Lingering Echoes

A word held back, a sigh too deep,
A silence stretched, too far to keep.
Unspoken truths, a hidden scar,
Carved in moments left ajar.
The weight of almost, heavy lies,
Lingering in unsaid goodbyes.
A thought withheld, a glance away,
Lost between what hearts won't say.
Yet in the hush of night's embrace,
Regret and longing trade their place.
For even words left in the past,
Find their way through time at last.

33. Beauty of Contentment

A quiet heart, a steady mind,
Peace in moments, love that's kind.
The joy of less, the grace of slow,
The art of simply letting go. No race to run, no fight to
win,
Just breathing deep and looking in.
The sun still shines, the moon still glows,
And life unfolds the way it knows.
Happiness is not a chase,
But finding light in every place.
Enough is here, enough is now,
A life fulfilled, no need to bow.
Contentment is a quiet grace,

34. Fire Alarm Within

Strength is quiet, steady, deep,
A silent oath our souls still keep.
Not in the thunder, not in the fight,
But in the faith to find the light.
Each fall, each tear, each aching scar,
Has shaped you into who you are.
Doubt may whisper, fear may call,
Yet rise, for you have seen it all.
The fire inside will never fade,
It grows in trials, unafraid.
You are stronger than you know,
Let your spirit rise and glow.

35. Becoming Whole

Not in pieces left behind,
But in the peace we choose to find.
Not in what the past still holds,
But in the stories yet untold.
Growth begins when we embrace,
The shifting tides, the changing space.
You are not lost, nor torn apart
You are the sum of a healing heart.
Each scar you bear, each path you tread,
Has led you here, not where you've fled.
Becoming whole is not to mend,
But to love yourself without an end.

36. The Path Along

Every turn won't show you why,
Every dream won't touch the sky.
Some roads are winding, long, and steep,
Yet hold the steps you're meant to keep.
The map you seek is drawn in time,
With every climb, with every sign.
Doubt may whisper, pull you back,
But forward is the only track.
Trust the pauses, trust the pace,
Life's not always meant to race.
What's waiting at the journey's end,
Is where your heart will learn to mend.

37. Weightless

You are not what slipped away,
Not the words you didn't say.
Some things fade, some things stay,
Yet life moves on in its own way.
Holding tight won't bring back time,
Nor make the stars in silence shine.
The past is light when left alone,
Not chains, but echoes softly grown.
Breathe in now, breathe out then,
Let the waves return again.
Not all endings come with pain,
Some just free you once again.